HURRICANES AND TORNADOES

NEWS FLASH

PHYSICAL & HUMAN GEOGRAPHY

EXPLORE PLANET EARTH'S MOST DESTRUCTIVE NATURAL DISASTERS.

PHOTO CREDITS

©2017
Book Life
King's Lynn
Norfolk PE30 4LS

ISBN: 978-1-78637-155-3

All rights reserved
Printed in Malaysia

A catalogue record for this book
is available from the British Library.

Written by:
Joanna Brundle

Edited by:
Charlie Ogden

Designed by:
Natalie Carr

HURRICANES AND TORNADOES

CONTENTS

Words that appear like **this** are explained in the glossary on page 31.

WHAT ARE HURRICANES?

Imagine this! You've been **evacuated** from your home to a shelter. Outside, very strong winds are uprooting trees and tearing down electricity cables. Heavy rain is hammering down on every surface. Thunder booms all around and lightning flashes across the cloud-filled sky. It's a hurricane!

Hurricanes are very powerful tropical storms that form over warm oceans. Strong winds spiral inwards and upwards as hurricanes move across the ocean. When hurricanes reach land, they can badly damage buildings, cause floods and kill many people.

Over 8,000 people were killed in the city Galveston, Texas, U.S.A, when a hurricane hit it in 1900. It was the deadliest hurricane ever to occur in the U.S.A.

This image was taken by a weather satellite in space and shows the spiral shape of a hurricane.

Hurricanes usually last over a week and happen in three main stages. The first stage brings fierce, stormy conditions and increasingly strong winds. In the second stage, the wind drops, the Sun shines and all appears calm. But don't be fooled! During the final stage, heavy rain and strong winds return and cause lots of damage.

Hurricanes get their names from one of six alphabetical lists of names. This means that the first hurricane each year will have a name that begins with 'A', second with 'B' and so on. If a hurricane causes serious damage or loss of life, that name is never used again and it is replaced with a different name starting with the same letter.

Hurricanes are also called cyclones and typhoons.

Can you spot the eye of this hurricane, which is off the coast of Florida, U.S.A.?

At the centre of a hurricane is an area called the eye. Strong winds swirl around the eye in thick clouds known as the eyewall, but the eye itself is calm. When the eye is directly overhead, blue skies and sunshine return for a short time.

HOW DO HURRICANES FORM?

Air that is warm naturally rises. As the warm air rises, colder air flows in to take its place. This creates wind. As oceans are warmed by the Sun, the water **evaporates** into **water vapour.** The water vapour is picked up by the wind and this warm, moist air rises, meets colder air and **condenses** to form towering clouds and thunderstorms. At the top of the storm, which can be as much as 15 km high, air is pushed out and over the top of the storm, away from the eye. Some of this air cools and falls back down through the eye of the hurricane.

Changes in the weather lead to areas of high air pressure and areas of low air pressure. High air pressure is when lots of air is squeezed together, like the air in a balloon. High air pressure always wants to move towards low air pressure. This is why all the air rushes out of a balloon when you let go of it.

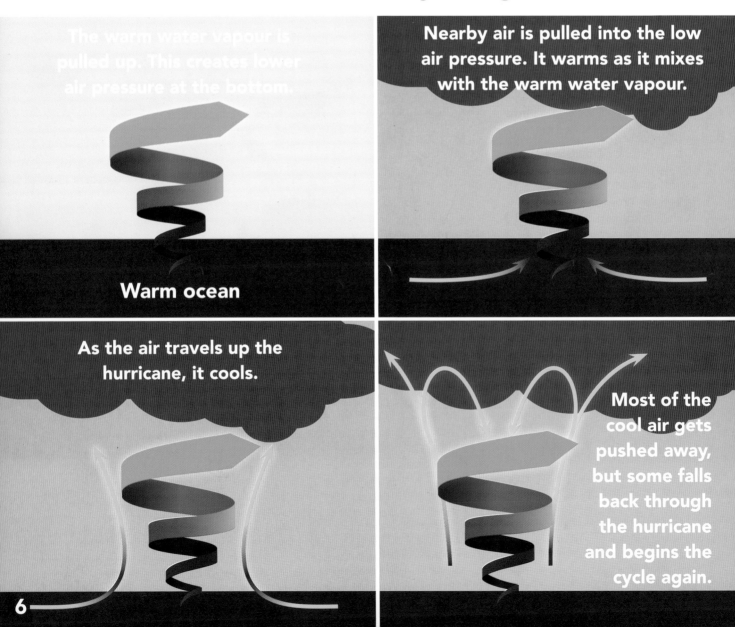

The warm water vapour is pulled up. This creates lower air pressure at the bottom.

Warm ocean

Nearby air is pulled into the low air pressure. It warms as it mixes with the warm water vapour.

As the air travels up the hurricane, it cools.

Most of the cool air gets pushed away, but some falls back through the hurricane and begins the cycle again.

As long as the storm stays over warm ocean water, the cycle will continue. Wind speeds will continue to increase and the storm will get bigger and stronger. When wind speeds reach 119 km per hour, the storm officially becomes a hurricane.

THE CORIOLIS EFFECT

The movement of the Earth spinning – or rotating – on its axis causes the winds to travel upwards in a spiral motion. This is called the Coriolis Effect. In the **Northern Hemisphere**, hurricanes spin in an anti-clockwise direction. In the **Southern Hemisphere**, they spin in a clockwise direction.

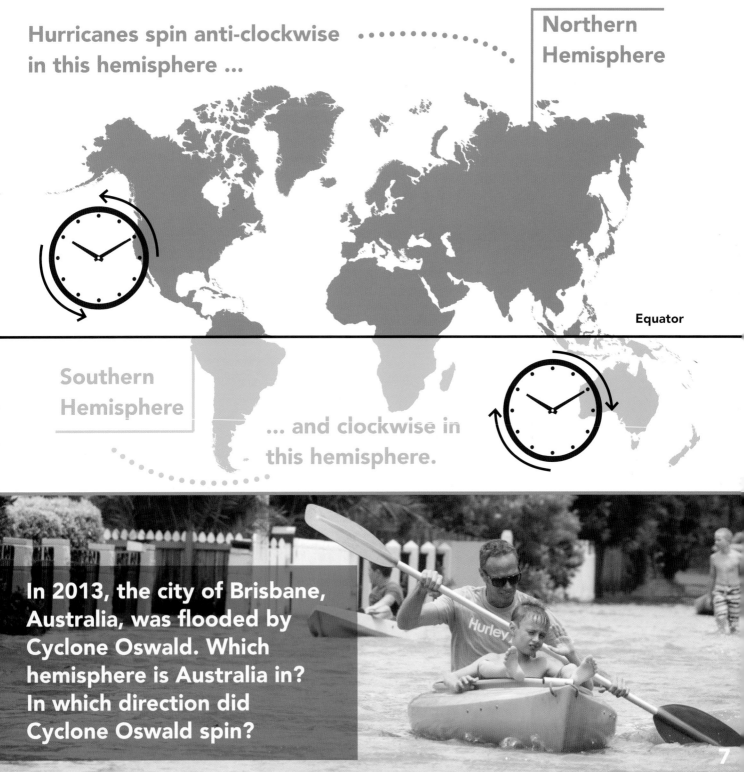

Hurricanes spin anti-clockwise in this hemisphere ...

Northern Hemisphere

Equator

Southern Hemisphere

... and clockwise in this hemisphere.

In 2013, the city of Brisbane, Australia, was flooded by Cyclone Oswald. Which hemisphere is Australia in? In which direction did Cyclone Oswald spin?

WHERE AND WHEN?

In order for hurricanes to form, the temperature of the sea must be at least 26 degrees **Celsius**. For this reason, hurricanes usually form over the hot, tropical oceans that lie either side of the **equator**. The arrows on the map show the directions in which they usually travel. Hurricanes do not form at the equator itself because the Coriolis Effect, which is needed to make a hurricane spin, is too weak at the equator.

Tropic of Cancer

Florida

Mexico

Haiti

Equator

Cuba

Tropic of Capricorn

Japan

Taiwan

Thailand

Bangladesh

Australia

When a hurricane reaches land or crosses cold water, it gradually fades away as it loses the energy supplied by the warm, moist, rising air.

A hurricane's wind speed increases rapidly as it approaches land.

Hurricanes usually occur during the hottest months of the year. However, different areas of the world are warm at different times. This means that different places in the world expect to see hurricanes at different times of the year. In the Eastern Pacific, the Gulf of Mexico and the Atlantic Ocean, hurricane season lasts from June to November. In the Western Pacific, typhoon season lasts from April to January. Cyclone season in the Indian Ocean lasts from April to December in the Northern Hemisphere and from November to April in the Southern Hemisphere.

Hurricanes can be very dangerous for aeroplanes due to their powerful winds and huge, thick clouds. An on-board radar helps pilots to avoid flying into hurricanes.

STORM SURGES

As a hurricane's winds spiral around, they force water on the surface of the ocean into the middle part of the storm. This creates a huge mound of water. When the hurricane hits land, this mound of water, known as a storm surge, crashes onto the shore and causes flooding.

Storm surges can be very powerful and often cause more damage and loss of life than the hurricane itself. In cities, they flood streets, homes and businesses. In the countryside, they cover farms, destroy the crops and damage the soil. The the flood waters can trigger **mudslides** and if it is **polluted**, the water can help to spread disease.

During Hurricane Ike, which hit the east coast of the U.S.A. in 2008, this lifeguard station in Pensacola, Florida, was submerged by a storm surge.

A storm surge combined with a **high tide** causes the most serious flooding. Computer programs that work out how big a storm surge will be allow scientists to **predict** how much damage a storm surge will cause when it hits the shore. These programs, called slosh models, take into account things like a storm's strength, its path, the tides and the shape of both the coast and the sea bed. The models help scientists to warn people about dangerous storm surges and to decide whether an area needs to be evacuated.

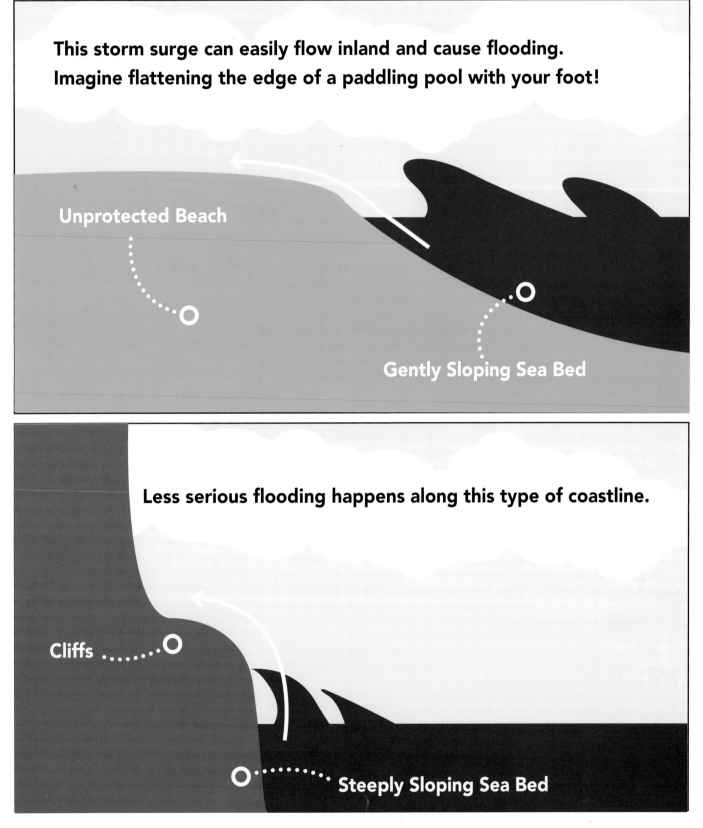

This storm surge can easily flow inland and cause flooding. Imagine flattening the edge of a paddling pool with your foot!

Unprotected Beach

Gently Sloping Sea Bed

Less serious flooding happens along this type of coastline.

Cliffs

Steeply Sloping Sea Bed

HURRICANE KATRINA 2005 AND CYCLONE SIDR 2007

On the 28th of August, 2005, an extremely powerful hurricane in the Gulf of Mexico began moving towards the southern coast of the U.S.A. This storm was called Hurricane Katrina and it caused a 10-metre-high storm surge that affected many different states. Louisiana, Mississippi, Florida, Georgia and Alabama were the worst affected.

Over 1,800 people died in Hurricane Katrina, many of them too sick or elderly to be evacuated before the hurricane struck. Around 80 percent of the city of New Orleans was flooded. Badly maintained levees, designed to protect the city from neighbouring Lake Pontchartrain, burst in over 50 places when the storm surge flooded into the lake.

Thanks to help from other countries, New Orleans has recovered and continues to hold its famous Mardi Gras carnival each year.

The country of Bangladesh has many cyclones and it is often badly affected by storm surges. The land is mostly at, or only just above, the level of the sea and it is has wide river **estuaries**, which allow flood water to rush inland. In November, 2007, Cyclone Sidr caused devastating damage along the entire length of Bangladesh's coastline. The blue arrow on the map shows the path of the cyclone.

Hurricanes tend to cause more damage and suffering in poor countries often have to such as Bangladesh. People in these countries use cheap, low-quality materials to build their homes, meaning that they can easily be destroyed by flooding, strong winds and heavy rains. They may not have transport to escape the flood waters or money to replace damaged food and equipment.

India

Myanmar

Bangladesh

Bay of Bengal

■ Area flooded by storm surge

This village in Bangladesh would be washed away by a storm surge.

WHAT ARE TORNADOES?

Tornadoes are giant columns of air that twist and spin at great speeds. They stretch from thunderclouds all the way to the ground.

The spinning motion of tornadoes means that they are sometimes called twisters.

Although they usually only last for a few minutes, tornadoes can cause serious damage, flattening houses and hurling cars hundreds of metres through the air. They act like giant vacuum cleaners, sucking up objects in their path. The biggest danger from tornadoes is being struck by flying **debris**.

This damage was caused by a tornado that hit Indiana, U.S.A., in 2012.

Hurricanes are usually hundreds of kilometres wide. Most tornadoes, however, are less than a kilometre wide. But despite being small in size, tornadoes can still pack a punch!

Like hurricanes, tornadoes also contain very strong winds. While the wind in a hurricane might reach a top-speed of about 320 km per hour, the winds that make up tornadoes often reach top-speeds of over 480 km per hour. That's about five times faster than a cheetah running at top-speed.

HOW DO TORNADOES FORM?

Most tornadoes are caused by thunderstorms, particularly supercell thunderstorms.

Supercell thunderstorms have very tall storm clouds and an anvil shape on top.

Supercell thunderstorms form when moist, warm air rises and meets dry, colder air to produce storm clouds. When these two different types of air travel in different directions and at different speeds, a fast-spinning column of air called a vortex may form. If this vortex makes contact with the ground, it is called a tornado.

Try this to understand why a tornado spins!

Hold a pen or pencil between your two hands. Your hands represent warm and cold masses of air. Move your hands in different directions. What happens?

Meteorologists are scientists who study the weather and try to understand why certain types of weather form. They also try to predict what types of weather will occur in the future. Tornadoes, however, continue to puzzle meteorologists, who still do not fully understand how they form. Until a tornado is very close by, it is impossible to tell exactly where it will strike, so people often have very little warning and time to prepare.

This man is building a tornado shelter with steps down to a concrete, underground chamber.

WHERE AND WHEN?

The most damaging tornadoes usually happen in places such as the U.S.A., Bangladesh and India. These places also have the highest number of tornadoes, but tornadoes also occasionally appear in South America, Australia and Europe. The central part of the U.S.A., known as the Great Plains, is the perfect place for tornadoes to form. Warm, moist winds from the Atlantic Ocean meet cold air drawn in from Canada. This area of the U.S.A. experiences so many tornadoes that it has been nicknamed Tornado Alley.

Canada

Montana

North Dakota

Minnesota

Wyoming

South Dakota

Nebraska

Iowa

Colarado

Kansas

Missouri

Atlantic Ocean

New Mexico

Oklahoma

Arkansas

Texas

Mississippi

Louisiana

Gulf of Mexico

■ **Rocky Mountains**

■ **Tornado Alley**

Tornadoes mostly form over land, but weak tornadoes can form over water. These are called waterspouts and they are most common the in the Gulf of Mexico. Waterspouts are actually just spinning columns of water vapour.

Tornadoes can occur at any time. During spring and early summer, however, wind patterns around the world change. These changing wind patterns cause a lot of tornadoes to occur at this time of year, which is why many people call spring and early summer "tornado season". Oddly, even though we don't know everything about how tornadoes form, we do know at what time of day tornadoes are most likely to occur – it is between three o'clock in the afternoon and nine o'clock in the evening. At this time of day, the land has had lots of time to be warmed by the Sun, causing warm air to rise.

Tornadoes frequently occur when hurricanes hit land. When Hurricane Ivan reached Alabama, U.S.A., in 2004, it caused 127 tornadoes in nine different states.

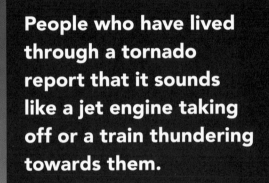

People who have lived through a tornado report that it sounds like a jet engine taking off or a train thundering towards them.

WHAT DO TORNADOES LOOK LIKE?

When tornadoes occur, there are normally very dark clouds in the sky. There may also be lightning in the sky at the same time. Most tornadoes have a funnel shape, which is narrow at the bottom and wide at the top. The narrow end that touches the ground is usually surrounded by dust and debris that has been sucked up by the tornado.

Sometimes, tornadoes have a narrow, rope-like shape, especially when they are beginning to slow down and to out.

Some tornadoes form the shape of a cylinder and are known as stovepipe tornadoes.

Tornadoes can appear in a variety of colours. If they have picked up little or no debris, they usually look grey or white.

Tornadoes that have picked up large amounts of dirt and debris often look dark and smoky.

A green tint to the sky can be a warning sign that a tornado is approaching.

Tornadoes in the Great Plains often look red because they have sucked up soil that , in some states, is reddish in colour. Tornadoes spin in the same direction as hurricanes – anti-clockwise in the Northern Hemisphere and clockwise in the Southern Hemisphere. Like hurricanes, they are thought to have a calm, clear 'eye' at their centre.

TERRIFYING TORNADOES

Although a tornado can happen as a single event, sometimes many tornadoes occur at the same time in what is known as a Super Outbreak. From the 25th to the 28th of April, 2011, the largest and most damaging Super Outbreak ever recorded affected 21 states in the U.S.A., from Texas in the south to New York in the north. Over the four days, around 350 different tornadoes were recorded, with 316 of these all occurring just on the 27th of April. Over 320 people died and around 2,275 were injured. Mississippi and Alabama were the worst affected states, with over 200 deaths being reported in Alabama alone.

These pictures show the serious damage caused in Alabama on the 28th of April 2011.

A Super Outbreak also occurred in the U.S.A. in 1974, with 148 tornadoes affecting 13 states.

Although tornadoes are most common in the U.S.A., they can happen anywhere in the world and people in the U.K. report around 30 each year. Most of these are very weak but on the 28th of July, 2005, a strong tornado with wind speeds of over 200 km per hour struck Birmingham. It uprooted hundreds of trees, damaged around 1,000 homes and injured around 20 people. It was caused by warm and very wet conditions that were being pushed northwards against much colder, drier air.

Birmingham

TRACKING AND MEASURING
HURRICANES AND TORNADOES

Special aeroplanes carrying radar and computer technology are often flown into the eye of a hurricane so that they can collect information about the temperature, speed and direction of the wind inside the hurricane. Scientific instruments that measure various things about hurricanes are also dropped inside the storms. These instruments are able to send back information about what the storm is like at different levels. All these measurements help scientists to find out where and when hurricanes are likely to strike.

The Saffir-Simpson Scale rates the power of hurricanes from 1 to 5 according to their wind speed and the damage they cause. A category 1 hurricane has wind speeds between 119 and 153 km per hour and causes minor damage, while a category 5 has wind speeds over 249 km per hour and can cause huge amounts of damage.

Some people, known as storm chasers, use fast cars to follow hurricanes and tornadoes. These cars carry scientific equipment that enables the storm chasers to study the hurricanes and tornadoes and to take close-up photographs of them. Some people make a living selling these photographs, but it's dangerous work!

Scientists measure the width of a tornado and the speed at which it is moving, but the most important measurement is how fast it is spinning. The faster a tornado spins, the more damage it can cause.

Despite all the information gathered by weather stations like this, scientists still cannot say exactly where or when a hurricane or tornado will strike.

In 1971, Professor Theodore Fujita invented the Fujita Scale to estimate the spin speed of a tornado based on the damage it caused. The scale goes from F0 to F5, F0 being the least damaging and F5 the most damaging. A category F1 tornado, with wind speeds from 117-180 km per hour, can push a car off the road, while a category F5 tornado can flatten houses and has a wind speed of more than 420 km per hour. In the U.K., a similar scale, called the TORRO scale, is used.

El Niño and La Niña are weather patterns that affect the flow of the ocean and the direction of the wind in some parts of the world. They arethought to have an effect on the power of hurricanes and on how often they happen.

WILDLIFE WINNERS AND LOSERS

Natural disasters like hurricanes and tornadoes can cause serious problems for plants, animals and the **habitats** that they live in. Tornado season, for example, happens when many birds are nesting and the tornadoes often lead to many nests being destroyed.

Fast winds can dislodge nests from trees.

In 2005, Hurricane Katrina destroyed five million acres of forest in Mississippi, Louisiana and Alabama. The habitats of many different plants and animals were damaged.

Plants and animals are, however, able to **adapt** to deal with tough weather conditions. Some have adapted so well that they actually benefit from these stormy conditions. Palm trees have adapted to be able to bend in the wind without breaking.

The high winds help plants whose seeds are carried by the wind, such as orchids, by spreading their seeds far and wide. Gopher frogs and spadefoot toads benefit from the rain as it makes large ponds where they can raise their young.

Uprooted trees provide shelter for mammals like black bears, while **scavengers** find new food sources amongst the debris.

Raccoons looking for food.

Coastal **wetlands** can help to reduce the flooding caused by hurricanes by absorbing heavy rains and storm surges. Wetlands like these are now being properly looked after so that their natural wildlife can return. They provide a habitat for many animal and plant species, such as sea turtles, fiddler crabs and geese.

Strong winds can even benefit humans! Although the town of Greensburg, Kansas, was destroyed by a tornado in 2007, its residents now make good use of the wind. A wind farm has been built that provides more than enough energy for all the homes and businesses in the community.

SURVIVING HURRICANES AND TORNADOES

If you are ever in an area where hurricanes and tornadoes are common, listen to the radio and television for warnings. Keep an eye on the sky and watch out for dark storm clouds. Listen for the rushing sound of an approaching tornado and if you spot a funnel shape in the sky, find shelter immediately. If you are outside, lay flat in a ditch with your arms covering your head.

Some areas have very loud tornado sirens that warn people when a tornado is coming.

It's not safe to be inside a car during a tornado!

Heading to a basement or hiding underneath a sturdy table can protect you from falling trees.

If there is a hurricane warning, make sure you bring inside any outdoor objects that could blow away and hurt others. Board up doors and windows and make sure that all pets are inside. Prepare a disaster supply kit including tinned food and a tin opener, bottled water, a battery operated torch and radio, in case power is lost, and warm, protective clothing. Make sure the family car is full of fuel in case you are instructed to evacuate your area in a hurry.

Roads quickly become blocked by thousands of people trying to escape to safety, so leave immediately if told to do so.

A hurricane or cyclone watch means that the storm is expected in a few days but a warning means it is expected within 24 hours.

FASCINATING FACTS

The Bermuda Triangle is an area of the Atlantic Ocean where many ships have disappeared without a trace. Some people believe waterspouts may be to blame.

The storms that create tornadoes can produce giant hailstones like these. The biggest ever recorded was 20 centimetres wide and weighed 900 grams. It fell in South Dakota, U.S.A., in July of 2010.

Hurricane John, which hit the East Pacific in 1994, holds the record for the greatest distance ever travelled by a hurricane – 13,280 kilometres. It also holds the record for being the longest lasting hurricane ever recorded at 31 days.

The word "hurricane" comes from the Spanish word "huracan", which probably came from the name of the Mayan god of storms, Hunraken.

The word tornado comes from the Spanish word "tornar", meaning "to turn".

GLOSSARY

adapt — change over time to suit different conditions

Celsius — a scale of temperature, divided into 100 degrees, in which 0 is the freezing point and 100 is and 100 the boiling point of water

condenses — changes from a gas or vapour into a liquid

debris — the pieces that are left when something has been destroyed

equator — an imaginary line around the surface of the Earth that is equal in distance from the North and South Poles

estuaries — the places where large rivers empty into the sea

evacuated — moved away from an area to escape danger

evaporates — turns from a liquid into a gas usually through heat

habitats — the natural environments in which animals or plants live

high tide — the highest level that sea water reaches up a beach

levees — banks built along a river or lake, to stop water flooding onto the land

mudslides — large amounts of mud that have fallen, or are falling, down hills or mountains

Northern Hemisphere — the half of the Earth that lies north of the equator

polluted — made poisonous or dirty by the actions of humans

predict — to say that an event will happen in the future

radar — a device that finds out the position of nearby objects using radio waves

satellite — a machine in space that travels around taking photos and transmitting information

scavengers — creatures that feed on rubbish or rotting material

Southern Hemisphere — the half of the Earth that lies south of the equator

supercell thunderstorms — the largest and most powerful type of thunderstorm, which produce hail, very strong winds and very heavy rain

water vapour — water that is in the form of gas and below the boiling temperature

wetlands — marshes, swamps, bogs or any areas of land where water covers the soil

INDEX